# Caring for the Earth

## The Environment, Christians and the Church

by
**Keith Innes**
Vicar of Doddington, Newnham and Wychling, Kent

### GROVE BOOKS LIMITED
Bramcote    Nottingham    NG9 3DS

## CONTENTS

|     |                                                                       | Page |
| --- | --------------------------------------------------------------------- | ---- |
| 1.  | Introduction                                                          | 3    |
| 2.  | Environmental Responsibility—The Ethical Issues                       | 6    |
| 3.  | Ecological Perspectives in Biblical Theology                          | 10   |
| 4.  | God, Humanity and Nature—Some Models from Recent Theological Thought  | 17   |
| 5.  | A Christian Response to Creation                                      | 21   |
| 6.  | *Faith in the Countryside* and Ecology                                | 23   |

Copyright Keith Innes 1987 and 1991

## ACKNOWLEDGMENTS

I am grateful to the Parishes of Alfold and Loxwood, and the Diocese of Guildford for enabling me to spend time studying the subject of this booklet, and to Dr. A. R. Peacocke of the Ian Ramsey Centre, Oxford, for his guidance and encouragement. Responsibility for the finished product of course remains entirely my own.

Some of the material in this Booklet is published in a different form by Farmington Institute in *Resources for a Green Theology*.

## PREFACE TO THE SECOND EDITION

I am grateful to Grove Books for the opportunity to revise the Booklet and update some of the references. I have also added a final section on the report *Faith in the Countryside*.

## THE COVER PICTURE

is taken from a photograph by Greg Forster—an unauthorized tip in Manchester's green belt!

## BIBLICAL QUOTATIONS

The quotations are taken from *The New English Bible* (Oxford University Press and Cambridge University Press; 1961, 1970).

*First edition* July 1987
*Second Edition* November 1991

**ISSN** 0951-2667
**ISSN** 1 85174 195 X

# 1. INTRODUCTION

Ecology is the study of the relation of living things to each other and to their environment. The term is used here mainly of human ecology, which means the relation between human beings and their works, and the rest of nature. The human species is totally and inescapably a part of nature. On the other hand, because of our intellectual powers we can also stand mentally outside the ecological processes, observing them as objects, and can manipulate them to our own ends. The combined effects of the accelerating increase in human population, and of the burgeoning growth in technology, multiply our capacity to affect the natural systems of which we are a part.

The ecological crisis has been described and summarized in many books and reports,[1] It manifests itself especially in the pollution of air, earth and water, and in the over-use and misuse of finite natural resources.

## (1) Pollution of the Air

The main sources of air pollution are industry, motor vehicles and the generation of electricity from fossil fuels. Sulphur dioxide from power stations and the oxides of nitrogen from motor vehicles can combine with atmospheric water to form acid rain which damages forests, and harms wildlife in lakes and rivers.

The discharge of carbon dioxide from electricity plants and motor vehicles also intercepts the earth's radiation of heat and increases the air temperature by the so-called 'greenhouse effect'. The increasing destruction of forests can exacerbate the problem by reducing the rate of natural removal of carbon dioxide. In this way climates may be affected, and, if a critical point is reached, the polar ice-caps may melt in summer.

The ozone region which protects the earth from the sun's dangerous radiations is threatened with depletion by chemical reactions arising from the exhausts of supersonic aircraft, and also from chlorofluorocarbons used in refrigerators, in the manufacture of expanded polystrene, and as propellants in aerosols.

Catastrophic pollution of the air can be caused by accidents at chemical plants. One such incident at Bhopal, India, in December 1984 resulted in large numbers of casualties. Radioactive leaks from power stations or other uses of nuclear energy may also result in untold damage, and may cover a virtually limitless area, as the recent (1986) disaster at Chernobyl

---

[1] For example Rachel Carson: *Silent Spring* (Penguin Books, Harmondsworth, 1965); *Man in his Living Environment* (Church Information Office, Westminster, 1970); Barbara Ward and Rene Dubos: *Only One Earth* (Penguin Books, Harmondsworth, 1972); Donella H. Meadows, Dennis L. Meadows, Jorgen Randers and William W. Behrens III: *The Limits to Growth* (Pan, London, 1974); *The Global 2000 Report to the President—Entering the Twenty-First Century* (Penguin Books, Harmondsworth, 1982); *The Conservation and Development Programme for the UK* (Kogan Page, London 1983); Norman Myers (ed.): *The Gaia Atlas of Planet Management* (Pan, London, 1985); *Our Responsibility for the Living Environment* (Church House Publishing, Westminster, 1986); Working Party for the Society, Religion and Technology Project: *While the Earth Endures: A Report on the Theological and Ethical Considerations of Responsible Land-Use in Scotland* (Edinburgh, 1986); Laurie Friday and Ronald Laskey (eds.): *The Fragile Environment: The Darwin College Lectures* (Cambridge University Press, 1989).

CARING FOR THE EARTH

showed. A nuclear holocaust would of course be the ultimate environmental disaster, rendering large parts of the earth's surface sterile, causing genetic mutations and possibly extinguishing all life.

## (2) Pollution of the Waters

Rivers are polluted by the discharge into them of untreated sewage, of the by-products of industry, and pesticides and fertilizers which drain or seep into them from the land. Eventually a river can become incapable of supporting life through the exhaustion of its oxygen. 30 tons of agricultural chemicals were washed into the Rhine during a fire at a chemical plant in Switzerland during 1986 and millions of fish died. Industries which use water as a coolant can cause 'thermal pollution' which results in the multiplication of some species of fish and the decrease or disappearance of others.

Polluted rivers of course pollute oceans, which, contrary to popular imagination, are finite both in their extent and in their capacity to deal with unwanted materials, and have no outlet. They are vital for all forms of life because of their ability to absorb and detoxify materials poured into them naturally from the land, because they provide oxygen through the operation of minute organisms called phytoplankton, and because they help to control the earth's temperature. The oceans are threatened not only by discharges via rivers, and sewage channelled directly into them, but also by the discharge of oil at sea, and by the dumping of toxic wastes. Both oceans and land are polluted by the polychlorinated biphenyls (PCBs) which have been used in industry since the 1930s and are highly toxic.

## (3) Pollution of the Earth

The soil is composed of inorganic matter derived from rocks, together with dead organic material, and is continually being produced. It can be polluted by poisonous or radioactive wastes. Its ability to sustain animal life can be impaired by the over-use of pesticides, especially the 'chlorinated hydrocarbons' such as DDT, dieldrin and endrin which concentrate in animal tissue higher in food chains than the pests which they are designed to eliminate. The effects of these poisonous substances may occur at a vast distance from the place of their original use. Some pesticides also contain substances such as compounds of mercury, arsenic and lead, which are persistent in their effects and are in the end lethal to wildlife.

## (4) The Earth's Resources

Estimating the extent of the earth's mineral reserves is notoriously difficult, but the fact remains that they are finite. Questions of the future availability of various minerals, especially fossil fuels, have a bearing on the world's supply of energy. Non-renewable energy sources such as oil, gas and coal do not exist in limitless quantities. Therefore every possible measure should be taken to prevent waste and reduce consumption. The use of renewable sources of energy would reduce the demands made on the earth's precious and irreplaceable minerals. These sources include hydroelectric processes, wind and water mills, tide power which can be harnessed where the difference between high and low water is

## INTRODUCTION

is sufficiently great, solar power, thermal energy from earth and sea, and wave power. Nuclear energy has often been hailed as the answer to humanity's future energy problems, but is subject to problems of cost, safety and the long-term disposal of radioactive wastes.

The oceans support a vast variety of animal life, from one-celled phytoplankton to fish and whales. The fishing industry supplies much of the world's protein, but over-fishing has depleted the stock of many kinds of fish.

The earth with its thin and uneven covering of soil is the basic resource for all life. It is at risk from over-cultivation which gives short-term benefits but may ultimately impoverish the earth. Overgrazing and the removal of trees and hedgerows lead to erosion. Tropical and sub-tropical soils are especially fragile. When tropical rain forests are felled, the soil is easily washed away, or baked hard by the sun, and the land becomes useless for agriculture.

In the Third World at least two billion people are said to use wood as their only fuel for cooking. The search for firewood often leads to the stripping of forests, with consequent erosion of the soil. When the search becomes fruitless, dung is sometimes burned instead, thus depriving the soil of a further means of enrichment. On the other hand if food is eaten uncooked disease spreads rapidly. This has been called the 'other energy crisis'.

The above are only a few examples of what Jürgen Moltmann judges to be 'the beginning of a life and death struggle for creation on the earth'.[1] The extinction of animals and the removal of plant species from the earth are also ecological issues, but space forbids their consideration here. Again, environmental question are inseparably intertwined with those of world development, peace and justice.[2] The ethics and politics of population control are also highly relevant but beyond the scope of this paper.[3] Our task here is a selective one: to isolate some of the underlying ethical issues and examine the bearing on them of the Bible and Christian theology. Finally we shall try to outline some of the kinds of practical response which are demanded of Christians today.

---

[1] Jürgen Moltmann, *God in Creation* (SCM, London, 1985), p.xi.
[2] The World Council of Churches has launched a process under the title 'Justice, Peace and the Integrity of Creation'. During 1989 a European Assembly was held at Basel, and in 1990 a World Congress took place at Seoul.
[3] Edward Echlin in *The Christian Green Heritage: World as Creation* (Grove Ethical Studies no. 74) proposes the idea of 'cosmic marriage', in which man and woman would regard as their family all creation, rather than just 'their own' children.

## 2. ENVIRONMENTAL RESPONSIBILITY—THE ETHICAL ISSUES

Questions about pollution and the conservation of resources are becoming increasingly important to large numbers of people, and are being more and more noticed by politicians. Nevertheless many environmentalists believe that no government has yet taken action sufficiently radical to address the issues adequately.

Behind the practical issues lie ethical questions, such as whether we have a responsibility for the earth; whether our responsibility for people is to our own generation alone, or to those of the immediate or remote future; what demands the undeveloped world makes on the richer nations, and whether these demands are valid, and so on. Such questions need to be examined, and to receive answers, before meaningful discussions and decisions can take place at the practical level. Here we shall mention two basic ethical issues: the value attaching to nature and, more briefly, our responsibility to others, especially to future generations.

### (1) The Value of Nature

The environment is only worth preserving if it is of value. The question of value divides itself into further questions, such as 'Valuable to whom?', 'Valuable as a whole or in all or some of its component parts?' and 'Are all species equally valuable?'

*(a) Valuable to Human Beings?* Our survival depends on a sufficient level of well-being in the soil, air and waters. If they are polluted beyond their ability to sustain life, the human race will die out. A serious depletion of the ozone layer in the atmosphere could allow fatal radiations from the sun to reach human beings, as well as other forms of life on earth. If all fuel reserves and other sources of energy prove inadequate for human needs, widespread suffering and death will result. In other words, our survival depends on the healthy operation of the rest of the biosphere. But, beyond mere survival, people need nature for the enjoyment of a full, rich and healthy life. For instance, the possibilities of intellectual enrichment are decreased when the removal of a species from the biosphere decreases the available field of study. The extinction of creatures which are beautiful diminishes our life aesthetically. In other cases our food resources may be reduced. Even where a natural entity does not seem directly to contribute to our well-being, it may do so indirectly as part of the food chain which sustains other creatures. Rocks, trees and mountains have also a symbolic value to men and women and have inspired art and poetry through the ages. On a spiritual level, many people find healing and renewal through the presence of natural entities which exist independently of their activities. On many levels, physical, mental and spiritual, therefore, our life is dependent on the natural environment. That is to say, our existence and well-being require the maintenance of that which has its being irrespective of ourselves and our efforts.

*(b) Valuable in itself?* Many people also feel that natural species, or the whole biosphere, have an importance and value apart from their significance for humanity. Can this intuition be supported by rational considerations?

## ENVIRONMENTAL RESPONSIBILITY—THE ETHICAL ISSUES

Tom Regan argues that animals, in common with human beings, have inherent value by virtue of the fact that they are 'the experiencing subjects of a life'.[1] Creatures which possess such value 'have an equal right to be treated with respect, to be treated in ways that do not reduce them to the status of things, as if they existed as resources for others.'

Lord Ashby suggests that a species is of value also as part of the evolutionary process.[2] Each one has taken millions of years to produce, and has within it unknown potentialities for future development. In part this point of view seems to rest on an analogy with the generally felt intuition that an object which has taken much time and ingenuity to produce, and especially one which possesses a high degree of complexity, is of more value than something into the production of which little time or thought has been put.[3] It is difficult to see that the argument would have any force without the existence of someone who expends, as it were, the time and ingenuity involved, and perhaps behind the idea of the preciousness of the evolutionary process lie hidden theistic assumptions. For the Christian, everything is of value because God created and sustains it, and the whole universe is within the scope of his redemptive purposes.

It is sometimes asked whether intrinsic value resides in each individual of a species, in the species as a whole, or in the whole ecosystem. It is probable that if value attaches to the whole, it attaches also to the parts. James E. Lovelock's 'Gaia hypothesis' suggests that 'the entire range of living matter on Earth, from whales to viruses, can be regarded as a single entity, capable of manipulating its environment to suit its needs'.[4] Each part of this marvellously complex system must also partake of some of the value attaching to the whole, because the whole depends for its healthy operation on each of the parts. And if each species is valuable, then every individual of the species must share in that value.

Yet there is need, in theory and especially in practice, to attribute greater intrinsic value to some natural entities than to others. Schumacher speaks of the Levels of Being, and of the 'jump' in values from minerals to plants, plants to animals, and animals to human beings.[5] Each level possesses the characteristics of levels below it, but has attributes which they do not. The additional value is conferred respectively by life, consciousness and self-awareness. A common intuition teaches us that the 'higher' levels *are* higher, that additional faculties and greater complexity constitute added value. It would be intolerable for most people to suppose that all things—rocks, trees, animals, viruses and people—are of equal value and have an equal right to consideration at all times.

It is widely felt that rarity also bestows value. Although every member of a valuable species partakes to some extent of its value, the last or a small number of surviving members possess 'rarity value'. If a rare book or piece

---

[1] Tom Regan, 'The Case for Animal Rights' in Peter Singer (ed.), *In Defence of Animals* (Basil Blackwell, Oxford, 1985), pp.21-24.
[2] E. Ashby, The Tanner Lecture on Human Values (University of Utah), April 4, 1979.
[3] Cf. W. H. Vanstone, *Love's Endeavour, Love's Expense* (Darton, Longman and Todd, 1977).
[4] N. Myers (ed.), *op. cit.,* p.100.
[5] E. F. Schumacher, *A Guide for the Perplexed* (Abacus, London, 1978), pp.24-35.

of porcelain is worthy of preservation, the same should be said of a rare plant or animal.[1]

## (2) Duties to Future Generations

In relation to pollution and the conservation of natural resources the question arises whether we have a responsibility to future generations or only to our own. Passmore argues that the claims of love urge us to consider our children and grandchildren.[2] The claim becomes less strong with succeeding generations. But Attfield points out that we now have power to affect the future for countless generations, for instance by leaving a legacy of radioactive wastes which may last up to a million years.[3] If we have the power to harm people in the far distant future, then we also have a duty to avoid doing them harm. The matter is complicated because we do not know for certain if there will *be* many future generations, if any, or what their needs will be. Future developments in technology may present them with a completely different set of advantages and disadvantages from ourselves. However the likelihood that there will be future people, and that their basic needs will be similar to our own, constitutes a sufficient reason for long-term reponsibility in handling the planet's resources. Attfield quotes Kavka's extension of a principle of John Locke so as to apply it to the earth. The Lockean principle states in connection with private property that each should leave enough and as good for others. Kavka's extension urges that we should 'use the earth's physical resources only to the extent that technology allows for the recycling or depletion of such resources without net loss in their output capacity.'[4] Renewable resources must be conserved, and non-renewable resources must only be used to the extent that technological innovations make their replacement possible. Since we do not know the details of the future, this appears to be the right way forward. Our responsibility towards future generations raises serious questions about the use of nuclear power, because of the possible genetic effects of radioactive leaks and the technical uncertainty surrounding the long-term storage of nuclear wastes.

## (3) Our Contemporaries

On the basis of the command to love our neighbours as ourselves it is clear that we have responsibilities to our contemporaries. Many of these contemporaries are starving and unable to improve their situation. Environmental degradation bears most heavily on the poor in Third World countries, and is often aggravated by the growing of cash crops to meet the demands of the 'developed' world.[5] The widespread indifference and ineffectiveness of the rich nations in remedying world hunger and

---

[1] Lord Ashby, *Reconciling Man with the Environment* (Stanford University Press, Stanford, California and Oxford University Press, Oxford, 1978), pp.84-85, quoted in A. R. Peacocke, *Creation and the World of Science* (Clarendon Press, Oxford, 1979) p.299.
[2] J. Passmore, *Man's Responsibility for Nature* (Gerald Duckworth and Co. Ltd., London, 1980).
[3] R. Attfield, *The Ethics of Environmental Concern* (Basil Blackwell, Oxford, 1983). I gladly acknowledge my debt to Passmore and Attfield throughout this chapter.
[4] Kavka, *The Futurity Problem*, quoted by Attfield, *op. cit.* p.107.
[5] See Sean McDonagh,*To Care for the Earth—a Call to a New Theology* (Geoffrey Chapman, London, 1986) pp.30-35; and *The Greening of the Church* (Geoffrey Chapman, London, 1990), pp.9-37)

## ENVIRONMENTAL RESPONSIBILITY—THE ETHICAL ISSUES

ecological deterioration constitute perhaps the greatest moral failure of the modern world.[1] Because the world is one, not only in the sense of being composed of interdependent nations but also in the ecological sense of being a single network of biological entities, the urgent claims of world development and economic reform cannot be separated from issues of pollution and resource depletion. The richer nations should limit their own consumption, and at the same time share both funds and expertise unconditionally with the undeveloped world. The poorer nations must also redress inequalities and injustices within their own borders. If these things are to happen a competent world authority, such as a greatly developed and strengthened United Nations, would seem to be necessary.[2]

---

[1] This is in spite of the widespread willingness of individual people in the West to raise funds for starving peoples in the Third World, shown by the success of Live Aid and other campaigns.

[2] Cf. The Brandt Report, *North-South: A Programme for Survival* (Pan, London, 1980), pp.257-266, and the Report of the World Commission on Environment and Development:*Our Common Future* (Oxford University Press, 1987) (The 'Brundtland Report').

## 3. ECOLOGICAL PERSPECTIVES IN BIBLICAL THEOLOGY

To what extent can an environmental ethic for today be derived from the Bible? The Christian tradition sees as central the events of sacred history: the call of Israel in the Old Testament and of the Church in the New, and above all the birth, life, death and resurrection of Christ. But it is equally important to see these events in the context of the creation of all things, the dependence of the universe on God, and the final redemption and fulfilment of the whole creation.

### (1) Creation in the Old Testament

Assessments of the role of creation in Old Testament thought have varied. Gerhard Von Rad asserted that the idea of creation was peripheral to the faith of Israel.[1] Israelite faith, he believed, was concerned only with the saving acts of God in her history. It was mainly in the Wisdom Literature that the doctrine of creation was an integral part of Israel's religion, and it was that literature which had most points of contact with the writings of other ancient near-eastern cultures, especially Egypt. Von Rad believed that creation played a subsidiary role in the parts of the Old Testament which were most genuinely Israelite. In Deutero-Isaiah, for instance, consideration of God as Creator is brought in to stimulate faith in God the Redeemer (Isaiah 40.25ff, 42.5, 43.1, 44.24, 54.5). Von Rad points out that in Psalm 89 creation is included in the acts of Yahweh's favour ($has^e$ $dê$ Yahweh, verses 1, 2) and in Psalm 74 creation is one of the saving acts of God (12-17). A similar pattern can be observed in Genesis, since Genesis 1 is part of a saving history which goes on to include the setting up of the Tent of Meeting, with its sacrificial ritual for the maintenance of right relationships between God and the people.

However, H. H. Schmid has shown that, far from being peripheral, 'Creation Theology' is 'The Broad Horizon of Biblical Theology'.[2] He points out that in Israel, as in other parts of the ancient Near East, 'Law, nature, and politics are only aspects of one comprehensive order of creation'. Offences against the just order ordained by God would be visited with natural and political punishments; when expiation was made, a whole and healthy state of affairs would be reinstated (Isaiah 40.1ff). Ideas like these lie behind the blessings and curses of the book of Deuteronomy, and the whole 'deuteronomic view of history'. One can see how the Plagues of Egypt, the destruction of Sodom and Gomorrah, and many other Old Testament incidents, fit into this framework. Other writers have drawn attention to the fact that, for the Old Testament, 'Nature is integrated into the moral order of Yahweh's government of mankind'[3] (Amos 7-8, Jeremiah 5.24-25, Hosea 8.7, 9.14, Joel 2.18-22). It is also important to notice that the gift of the land was an essential part of

---

[1] Gerhard Von Rad: *The Problem of the Hexateuch and other Essays* (SCM, London, 1984) pp.131-134.
[2] H. H. Schmid: 'Creation, Righteousness, and Salvation: 'Creation Theology' as the Broad Horizon of Biblical Theology', in B. W. Anderson (ed.): *Creation in the Old Testament* (SPCK, London, 1984).
[3] J. L. McKenzie: *A Theology of the Old Testament* (New York: Geoffrey Chapman, 1974) p.199; cf. E. C. Rust: *Nature and Man in Biblical Thought* (Lutterworth Press, London, 1953) pp.50-55.

God's covenant with Israel.[1] Walther Eichrodt writes:
'By making possession of the land dependent upon faithfulness to the covenant God includes Man's relation to Nature within the sphere of responsible human behaviour, and impresses upon him his distinctive position in the world of creatures. His sin means that the land is defiled, and the same land will vomit forth the nation which has become untrue to its moral responsibility.'[2]
The doctrine of creation may thus be seen as the framework within which the work of God in saving power can be understood.

The account of creation in Genesis 1.1-2.3 declares that everything is originated by God and is dependent on him for its continued existence. The creation is the result of God's unilateral action. With each stage of the drama the earth becomes more orderly and habitable. Light is separated from darkness, the upper waters from the lower, the earth from the seas. The earth produces plants and trees, the seas produce living creatures and birds, and later the earth also brings forth animals, but the living creatures are also said to be created by God—they are not the unaided offspring of the earth and seas. The human being is made in God's image and given authority over the world of nature. God's blessing is given to the inhabitants of the sea and the air, and later to human beings, and they are given authority to procreate and fill the earth (no blessing is given to the land animals, but this may be due to stylistic considerations—they share the sixth day with humanity). The food of human beings and of all living creatures is vegetarian. At the end of his work God rests, by contrast with the deities of Mesopotomia and Canaan who were engaged in an annual cycle of life, conflict and death to which the community, through its cultus, was connected. Moltmann has emphasized the importance of the Sabbath as marking the completeness of God's creation. He points out that the Sabbath, and not humanity, is the 'crown' of creation.[3]

The sun, moon and stars, which possess the character of semi-divine beings in the myths of other nations, are in Genesis 1 given merely to mark times and seasons. In the Old Testament, therefore, the myth of creation is brought under the control of Israel's monotheistic faith.

In the final form of Genesis this creation story is followed by another which focuses attention on the relationships of the human being with the earth and the animals, and on the institution of marriage. In Chapter 1 the human being shares his earthly home with the other creatures, and in Chapter 2 their life in their shared habitation receives closer attention (2.4-25). The human being is formed from the dust of the ground, and put in the garden of Eden to till and care for it. He names the animals, but because none of them is suitable as a companion for him, God makes the woman from one of his ribs.

---

[1] See H. Paul Santmire: *The Travail of Nature* (Philadelphia: Fortress Press, 1985) pp.190-192, and other writers there referred to.
[2] Walther Eichrodt: *Theology of the Old Testament* (London: SCM, 1967) Vol. 2, p.119.
[3] J. Moltmann: *op city.* pp.6, 31, 197. See also his *Creating a Just Future: The Politics of Peace and the Ethics of Creation in a Threatened World* (SCM, London, 1989), pp.61-66, 80-87.

CARING FOR THE EARTH

It has often been noted that the story of creation in Genesis 1 cannot be separated from that of the Flood, where the forces of chaos, which had been driven back in creation, again overwhelm the earth. However, God makes a new beginning by means of the 'ecological covenant' with Noah, his family and every living creature. Human beings are now given permission to eat meat, but the value of life is safeguarded by the prohibition of eating the blood. The rainbow becomes a sign of God's promise never again to devastate the earth by a flood. (Genesis 9.1-17).

The concept of creation in other parts of the Old Testament is in general agreement with the two Genesis myths. In Psalm 104, which has been found to have links with ancient Egyptian literature, the human being takes his place beside other creatures in the world of nature. Psalm 93 speaks of the power of God as King, establishing the world and overcoming the forces of chaos. Psalm 8 combines a sense of awe and mystery before creation, with a declaration of the authority given to human beings. In the hymn which forms the first part of Psalm 19 the universe bears witness to God; the second section, which has been added, concerns the goodness and benefits of the Law of the Lord.

Creation is also in the background of the prophetic oracles (eg Jeremiah 5.22-23, 27.5, 32.17, Amos 5.8-9). And in the Wisdom Literature creation, judgment and morality are bound together, as for example:
'A man who sneers at the poor insults his Maker,
and he who gloats over another's ruin will answer for it.' (Prov. 17.5).

Proverbs also contains the statement that 'a righteous man cares for his beast' (12.10), and similar sentiments are implied in Job's protestation:
'If my land has cried out in reproach at me,
and its furrows have joined in weeping,
if I have eaten its produce without payment
and have disappointed my creditors,
may thistles spring up instead of wheat,
and weeds instead of barley!' (Job 31.38-40).

Wisdom personified was instrumental in creation and is built into the structure of the universe. Yet she is accessible to the person who fears the Lord (Proverbs 8-9), even though Wisdom is beyond his direct understanding (Job 28). The wisdom of King Solomon included an understanding of nature (1 Kings 4.33). The precise observation of nature is a feature of the Book of Proverbs (e.g. 30.24-31), where wisdom involves both devotion and intellectual understanding. The figure of Wisdom personified prepares the way for the New Testament idea of the Word of God (John 1.1-14) who was instrumental in creation, yet became flesh in the Incarnation.

The Old Testment is, then, full of assertions of the dependence of all things on God and of God's activity in and through nature. Attention to nature is thus seen as part of the fear of the Lord.

**(2) The Value of Nature in the Bible**
The Old Testament law codes include provision for the protection and safeguarding of non-human creatures. The land was to be allowed to lie fallow every seventh year as a 'sabbath of sacred rest'(Leviticus 25.4).

Every fifty years, on the Day of Atonement in the Jubilee Year, all land must return to its original owner. No one had unconditional rights over the land, because it belonged to the Lord (Leviticus 25.23). It was forbidden to take a mother bird with her young (Deuteronomy 22.6-7) An ox was not to be muzzled while it was treading out the corn (Deuteronomy 25.4). In harvesting the crops, the rights of the owner were recognized, but he was to reap in such a way that something was left for others who were without resources of their own (Deuteronomy 23.24-25, 24.19-21). Consideration was thus to be extended both to the neighbour and to other creatures. A cow or sheep was not to be slaughtered for sacrifice at the same time as its young, and a young animal was not to be taken from its mother before seven days old (Leviticus 22.27-28). Trees which bore fruit for food were not to be cut down in time of siege (Deuteronomy 20.19-20). In the Holiness Code, fruit from the newly-planted trees was not to be eaten for three years. In the fourth year it was to be offered to God (Leviticus 19.23-25). Thus the people would be reminded that all fruit was the Lord's, and was given to humans on his terms.

The New Testament continues in this traditon. Jesus in Luke 13.15, 14.5 assumes that people have a humane attitude to their domestic animals. (St. Paul in 1 Corinthians 9.9 applies Deuteronomy 25.4 to preachers not oxen, but he may merely be making an exegetical point!) The parables of Jesus, and his observations regarding animals and plants (Matthew 6.26-30), show that he valued the earth and living creatures. But the Incarnation itself, in which God entered into the ecological process in person, is the most powerful evidence of the value of the world to God.

### (3) Immanence and Transcendence
God in the Old Testament is distinct from creation and sovereign over it, but is also present and active within it. He reveals himself in terms of natural forces, especially in the storm (e.g. Psalms 29.3-9; 77.16-20). We have seen that the operations of nature were understood to be instrumental in fulfilling God's purposes for Israel and for other nations. This tension and balance, between God as sovereign over nature and outside it, and yet active within it, runs right through the Bible. According to the Synoptic Gospels Jesus taught that God was both the Creator (Mark 10.6) and Sustainer (Matthew 6.26-30) of the world, and made his sun rise on good and bad alike (Matthew 5.45). St. Paul held that the created order held clues, for those with eyes to see them, to God's power and character (Romans 1.20). All things come from God the Father, and have their existence through Jesus Christ (1 Corinthians 8.4-6). For the writer to the Hebrews 'the universe was fashioned by the word of God, so that the visible came forth from the invisible' (11.3). Yet in words attributed to St. Paul, the Acts of the Apostles can say that in God 'we live and move, in him we exist' (Acts 17.27).

If we enquire more closely into the character of God's presence within nature, there is some evidence that the people of the Old Testament saw nature as possessing a sort of diffuse psychic consciousness. E. C. Rust draws attention to the 'chain of psychic responses' in Hosea 2.21-22 including Israel, the earth and its products, and God.[1] There appears to be

---
[1] E. C. Rust, *Nature and Man in Biblical Thought* (London, 1953).

CARING FOR THE EARTH

a diffused consciousness which can be indwelt and used by Yahweh. In the same vein Pedersen wrote, 'The earth is a living thing. It has its nature, with which man must make himself familiar when he wants to use it; he must respect the soul as it is, and not do violence to it in appropriating it.'[1] This kind of thinking probably lies behind the 'Covenant Lawsuit' passages where earth and heavens, mountains and hills are called upon to bear witness to human wickedness (Micah 6.1-2, Isaiah 1.2, Psalm 50.4, Job 20.27, Deuteronomy 4.26, 30.19, 31.28, 32.1).[2]

In the New Testament the concept of the 'Cosmic Christ' through whom all things are sustained and kept in existence (John 1.1-4, Hebrews 1.1-3, Colossians 1.16-17) also asserts a divine presence within nature. The Incarnation may be seen as a unique intensification or focus of God's immanence in creation. Christ as the Second Adam (Romans 5.14-17, 1 Corinthians 15.45-49) constitutes a new beginning for humanity.

## (4) The Dominion of the Human Species

In Genesis 1 God directs the human being to rule the other creatures. He charges him, 'Be fruitful and increase, fill the earth and subdue it, rule over the fish in the sea, the birds of heaven, and every living thing that moves upon the earth' (Genesis 1.28). It has been asserted that this charge implies a ruthless, exploitative attitude towards nature, and indeed that the Judaeo-Christian tradition, stemming from this charge, is responsible for the present ecological crisis.[3] But, as James Barr has pointed out, the imagery of Genesis owes much to the oriental idea of the shepherd king, who is totally responsible for the welfare of his subjects as well as exercising authority over them.[4] J. A. Baker speaks of the use of 'cosmic iconography' to express the status of the King in the Ancient Near East[5]. In Egypt the Pharaoh was named 'the image of Amun-Re'. In Psalm 72 God is asked to endow the king with his own righteousness, so that the people may enjoy justice and prosperity. It is to be noted also that in Genesis 2 the role of the human being in caring for the earth and the animals is at least as prominent as his authority. The word *kbs* translated 'subdue' in Genesis 1.28 is indeed a violent word—it is used of forcing people into slavery (Jeremiah 34.11, 16, 2 Chronicles 28.10, Nehemiah 5.5), of rape (Esther 7.8) and conquering people and lands in war (Numbers 32.22, 29, Joshua 18.1, 2 Samuel 8.11, 1 Chronicles 22.18). But as James Barr states, it is used in Genesis in relation to the earth, not the animals, and should be interpreted as applying to settlement and agriculture. There is a change after the Flood, when for the first time mention is made of the fear felt by animals towards human beings and people are allowed to eat meat. But even then restraint is provided by the prohibition of eating meat with the blood. Human authority therefore must still be exercised with responsibility. We are stewards rather than owners.

[1] J. Pederson, *Israel* I-II (Oxford University Press, London, 1926), p.155.
[2] See Keith Innes, 'The Witness of Nature' in *New Fire* Vol. VIII, No. 64, Autumn 1985, pp.418-420.
[3] E.g. Lynn White, Jr., 'The Historical Roots of our Ecologic Crisis', *Science*, 155 (1967) pp.18-30.
[4] James Barr, 'Man and Nature—The Ecological Controversy and the Old Testament' in *Bulletin of the John Rylands Library* 55 (1972) pp.9-32.
[5] J. A. Baker, 'Biblical Attitudes to Nature' in H. Montefiore (ed.), *Man and Nature* (Collins, London, 1975) p.92.

## (5) The Fall

Genesis 3 contains the story of humankind's primordial act of disobedience towards God, leading to fear, suffering and dislocated relationships. The ground is accursed on his account, so that he can get food from it only by laborious toil, and his life in the Garden comes to an end. The following chapters tell of increasing violence: Cain kills Abel, Lamech threatens unlimited vengeance (4.23-24). Eventually the whole earth was full of violence (6.13). Nature has become an enemy to humanity (Genesis 3.17.19) and, after the Flood, humanity has become nature's enemy also (9.2).

In the New Testament St. Paul accepts the story of the Fall apparently as historical fact (Romans 5.12-19, cf. 1 Timothy 2.13-14). In Romans 8.18-25 he also seems to speak of the universe as being dependent for its own freedom upon the complete liberation and glory to be experienced by God's human children. 'The created universe waits with eager expectation for God's sons to be revealed'. These words have often been taken to imply a 'Cosmic Fall'.[1] It is however possible that the word *ktisis* translated 'created universe' means here 'creature', so that the reference is to men and women themselves, and St. Augustine is said to have taken it in this sense.[2] In support of this interpretation E. Brunner argues 'It is not the creation which is "fallen" but man; the revelation in the creation has not been destroyed but by sin man perverts into idolatry that which God has given him.'[3] Similarly Adolph Schlatter writes: 'Our rebellion leads only to the corruption of our human will, not of nature, not God's work.'[4]

The scientific view of the development of the world also seems not to leave room for a cosmic 'Fall' as a historical event. The 'curse' of Genesis 3 expresses the connection between people's disrupted relationships with God and with each other, and their failure to live harmoniously with the natural environment. The fact that we so often experience nature as an enemy can rightly be seen as a judgment from God. The threat to our own welfare and that of the entire ecosystem is the form in which the 'curse' comes home to us today.

## (6) Renewal

Psalms 96.11-13, 98. 7-9 speak of the joy of all created things at the coming of the Lord to judge, and Isaiah 11.1-9 speaks of the future Messianic Age in terms reminiscent of the Garden of Eden (cf. Isaiah 49.5-13, 65.17-25, 66.22-23). Revelation 21-22 unfold the vision of the new heaven and earth. This concept, first found in Isaiah 65.17, 66.22, is also echoed in 2 Peter 3.13. All of these texts hold out the promise of a future for a redeemed material creation. St. Paul's exposition of the 'spiritual body' (1 Corinthians 15.35-49) implies not a purely

---

[1] Cf. Calvin's statement that the sin of Adam 'Perverted the whole order of nature in earth and heaven' quoted in *Our Responsibility for the Living Environment*, p.22.
[2] See H. Paul Santmire, *op. cit.* p.66.
[3] *Revelation and Reason* (London, 1947) quoted by Matthew Black, New Century Bible Commentary *Romans* (Marshall, Morgan and Scott, London, 1981), p.121.
[4] *Die Christliche Ethik* (Stuttgart, 1929) p.137, quoted in Klaus Bockmuhl, *Conservation and Lifestyle* (Grove Books, London, 1977).

spiritual, incorporeal existence in the future life, but resurrection to a new form of physical being, perfectly responsive to the spiritual life. It is of course impossible for us to visualize exactly the nature of the new heaven and earth, or of our new bodies (although the post-resurrection body of Jesus may give us some clues). The point is that there will be continuity with, as well as difference from, the present.

H. Paul Santmire points out that apocalpytic thought, which Jesus inherited, was essentially world-affirming, and anticipated not the destruction, but the renewal of heaven and earth.[1] He suggests that the parables of growth imply this future transformation.

It is also important to notice the reference in Matthew 19.28 to the eschatological 'rebirth' *(palingenesia)* which the New English Bible translates 'the world that is to be'. Returning to Revelation 21-22, the 'earthed' character of the future hope is further underlined by Revelation 22.1-5. This passage echoes Ezekiel 47.1-12, and describes the river of the water of life which brings healing to the nations, and the tree of life (cf. Genesis 2.9) on either side of the river.

In Colossians 1.20 'all things' are said to be included in the reconciliation wrought through Christ, and similarly in Ephesians 1.10 'all things' will be included in the unity which Christ brings *(anakephalaiosasthai)*.

Santmire points out that the earth-affirming character of the majority of the New Testament writings seems to be lacking in the Fourth Gospel, and in Hebrews which appears to promise a purely spiritual fulfilment of God's promises (see Hebrews 11-12).[2] This difference may be accounted for by supposing that these books start with a different perspective. They are concerned with deliverance through Christ from the sin and imperfection of the present age, rather than with the future of the earth as such. In other words they focus on the discontinuity rather than the continuity between this age and the next.

Moltmann observes that the new creation in the New Testament corresponds to the original creation in the Old, and is a mirror-image of it.[3] Whereas the 'protological' creation starts with the creation of the world and leads on to the appearance of human beings, the eschatological creation starts with the liberation of human beings and ends with the redemption of nature.

The strands which compose the biblical literature thus bear their varied witness to God as the creator and sustainer of all things, caring for nature and present within it, and charging women and men to care for it. The Bible also contains the promise of an unlimited future (in some form) for heaven and earth, in the redemptive purposes of God.

---

[1] H. Paul Santmire, *op. cit.*, p.200.
[2] *Ibid.*, pp.210-215.
[3] J. Moltmann, *op. cit.*, p.68.

## 4. GOD, HUMANITY AND NATURE—SOME MODELS FROM RECENT THEOLOGICAL THOUGHT

Scripture is the form in which God's revelation has become fixed in writing. Compared with other forms of revelation it has a distinctive quality of clarity and objectivity. It is true that no one theology of nature can be derived from the Bible. It is precisely the variety and many-sidedness of the biblical documents which make them an appropriate source from which to quarry resources for Christian thought and action. The work of biblical theology is to assess the appropriate weight to give to each facet of the biblical witness to God, to seek for links and interrelations between them, and to discern which aspects and relations should be drawn out to meet each situation, need or problem.

The biblical material stands near the source of the Christian tradition. Although the stream of that tradition nourishes and gives rise to varieties of authentic manifestations of Christianity as it passes through many different cultures and eras, ideas which are inconsistent with the Bible must be rejected as not belonging to the tradition. Indeed the tradition must be scrutinized, and is also to be sifted by controversy and conflict, in order to rid it of intrusive elements. This is no easy task, or even one which is ever completely fulfilled. Those who are assured that they hold and teach the whole biblical message are likely to be those whose assumptions and built-in processes of selection are most unconscious. The biblical witness needs to be moulded and interpreted for each generation and situation, but the biblical categories of thought must be distinguished from, and given priority over, just as they must be brought into dialogue with, structures of thought and experience in the surrounding culture.

The following is a very brief summary of some models or analogies used in recent theological writing about God, humanity and nature, and an attempt to indicate how they might be assessed in the light of this concept of biblical theology. Many of these models are referred to in the Anglican symposium *Man and Nature* (1975) which wisely prefaces them with the caution that none should be given a monopoly of our thinking, but that they are best allowed to modify each other.

### (1) Sovereignty and 'Making'

The models of sovereignty and 'making' emphasize God's otherness and transcendence. God by sovereign fiat causes all things to be. This traditional Christian model has been stated in recent times by Barth and his successors. It is the most obvious conception of creation in the Bible. It carries with it the corollary that the creation is quite external to and separate from God. It has become 'disenchanted' and 'desacralized', and can therefore be studied and manipulated without fear. This freedom must be balanced with the idea that human beings are God's stewards, with a responsibility to care for God's evolving handiwork with reverence and respect. The lack of this limitation has opened the way to the unbridled exploitation of nature which we see today.

## (2) Models based on God's Immanence

The Christian tradition also teaches that God is immanent in his creation, present within it and as it were creating it from within. J. V. Taylor speaks of creation in terms of 'life-giving energy and inspiration.' He quotes Julian of Norwich as saying, 'We are all in him enclosed, and he is enclosed in us!'; and goes on to write:

> 'The Spirit of Life is ever at work in nature, in history and in human living, and wherever there is a flagging or corruption or self-destruction in God's handiwork, he is present to renew and energise and create again.'[1]

Moltmann, also, emphasizes the importance of God's immanence for an ecological doctrine of creation today.[2] Rex Ambler suggests that God should be viewed as 'the ultimate reality that impinges on us.' At the present time we should see him in the pressures urging us to take responsibility for the future of the world.[3]

*Man and Nature* cites the analogies of the artist whose creation is both external to himself, and yet is also almost an extension of his personality, and of a garment (cf. Psalm 104.2) which both expresses and is separate from the identity of the wearer. Attention is also drawn to the biblical images of the Wisdom of God and his Word, which are almost emanations of his being, and are his agents in creation. A. R. Peacocke suggests that the relation between God and the world is analogous to the relation between our mind and body.[4] Sallie McFague further develops the model of the world as God's body.[5]

## (3) Unity

The Eastern Church has always emphasized the unity between God and creation. Maximus the Confessor (580-662) taught that humanity was to be thought of as mediator between God and the cosmos. This teaching suggests that the human being represents the whole of creation like a priest. This status of human beings is not their own achievement but is made possible by Christ. Maximus the Confessor regards incarnation as an event wider than the historical Incarnation of Christ. 'The Word of God, who is God, wills at all times and in all things to work the mystery of his incarnation'.[6] One of the heirs of this Christian tradition, Vladimir Solovyev (1853-1900) has made much of the image of *sophia* (wisdom) as standing at once for the whole of creation, humanity and the Church in space and time. He wrote:

> 'What is needed in the first instance is that we should treat our social and cosmic environment as an actual living being with which we are in the closest and most complete inter-action, without ever being merged in it.'[7] 701

---

[1] J. V. Taylor, *Go-Between God* (SCM, London, 1972).
[2] Moltmann, *op. cit.*, p.14.
[3] Rex Ambler: *Global Theology: The Meaning of Faith in the Present World Crisis* (SCM, London, 1987).
[4] A. R. Peacocke, *Creation and the World of Science* (Clarendon Press, Oxford, 1979), pp.133-135.
[5] Sallie McFague: *Models of God: Theology for an Ecological Nuclear Age* (SCM, London, 1987).
[6] Quoted by A. R. Peacocke, *op. cit.*, p.289
[7] Quoted in Paulos Gregorios, *The Human Presence* (World Council of Churches, Geneva, 1978).

Paulos Gregorios refers to God as 'the Wholly Other who presents himself to us through the created universe'. He pleads for 'participatory union, in and with Christ, with the *energeia* of God as it gives existence to us and to all other reality in creation.'

### (4) Nature as Sacrament

Gregorios teaches that

'This union with God and with each other in Christ is the true meaning of the eucharist, and the only authentically Christian mysticism. This eucharistic union-mysticism, in which we are one with the whole creation in our responsive self-offering to God, is the mystery that fulfils human existence.'[1]

The self-offering of Christ on the Cross, and God's gift of salvation to humankind in him, are rightly seen in classical Anglican thinking as the central reality of the Eucharist. Our priestly function in relation to creation, involving it with ourselves in self-offering to God, can nevertheless be affirmed in a responsive sense.

A. R. Peacocke urges the extension of the sacramental principle to all nature. The use of wine, bread and water as in some sense vehicles of God's grace in Holy Communion and Baptism implies that nature has both an instrumental function in fulfilling God's purpose, and also a symbolic function in revealing God to us. The same dual function underlies Christ's use of parables. God is to be found 'in, with and under' not only the elements of bread and wine but also the whole created order.[2] Philip Sherrard also, believing that the Greek Fathers of the Church hold the key to a truly Christian idea of the relation of humanity to nature, calls for a recovery of the sacramental view of nature.[3]

### (5) Teilhard de Chardin; Christian Pantheism?

Teilhard de Chardin (1881-1955) was a French Jesuit, biologist and palaeontologist. He believed that all creation has a psychic aspect or rudimentary consciousness. All things are evolving towards a great consummation to be fulfilled at the Omega Point, and this Omega Point coincides with the glorified Christ. This fulfilment is purely spiritual; matter is important only as a stage in the evolution of the universe towards a time when Christ's purely spiritual body will be the only reality. Teilhard's vision therefore seems to lack the biblical promise of a redeemed and renewed physical universe.[4]

Teilhard also points out that, through the scientific discovery of evolution, evolution has become conscious of itself. There is a sense in which the whole process of evolution now passes through us and depends on us. In view of the powers which human beings now have to control the future

---

[1] Paulos Gregorios, *op cit.*
[2] In *Man and Nature* (ed. H. Montefiore) pp.132-142, and *Creation and the World of Science* pp.290-291.
[3] Philip Sherrard: *The Rape of Man and Nature: An Enquiry into the Origins and Consequences of Modern Science* (Golgonooza Press, Ipswich, 1987).
[4] See H. Paul Santmire: *op. cit.* pp.155-171.

evolution and even survival of other species, this statement is no exaggeration.[1] Sean McDonagh makes considerable use of the Teilhardian vision, although he also draws on a variety of Biblical material as well as examples from the later Christian tradition.[2]

### (6) Process Theology—Panentheism

The term 'Pan-en-theism' has been coined to convey the idea that everything is in some sense in God, although God is greater than the sum-total of everything that is not God. Ian Bradley believes that the doctrine of panentheism is fully consistent with Scripture.[3] It especially characterises the process theologians. By believing that God has chosen to take the uncertain outcome of the life of created things into his own being, they make God vulnerable and not omnipotent. They see God as persuading and influencing created entities, and not as compelling them. However they also draw a distinction between God's primordial nature and his consequential nature, between his essence and his experience. Like Teilhard and his successors the process-theologians attribute an inner, psychic aspect to all creatures from molecules to mammals. All natural entities have 'feeling', although only the higher animals make conscious choices, and humanity has the capacity to reflect, and synthesise lower feelings.[4] In process thinking and Teilhardian views of the world, creation and redemption tend to become two aspects of one unceasing activity of God. Indeed Moltmann asserts that process theologians have no doctrine of creation, but only of God's preservation and ordering of the world.[5] However the belief that God is responsible for the existence as well as the development of the world is a basic Christian tenet. Nor can Biblical faith dispense with the sovereignty of God, however uncomfortable this idea may be at a time when the part played by chance in the development of the world is increasingly realized, and when authority of any kind is under attack. Only by struggling with the tensions between the strands of Biblical thought, and between them and our life today, can we preserve the integrity of our inheritance of faith and present a Christian message to a world in crisis.[6]

---

[1] Teilhard de Chardin, *The Phenomenon of Man* (Collins, London, 1965).
[2] Sean McDonagh: *To Care for the Earth: A Call to a New Theology* (Geoffrey Chapman, London, 1986) and *The Greening of the Church (1990)*.
[3] Ian Bradley: *God is Green: Christianity and the Environment* (Darton, Longman and Todd, London, 1990).
[4] *Anticipation* No. 25 (January 1979); see also No. 16 (March, 1974).
[5] Moltmann, *op. cit.*, p.79.
[6] Moltmann gives us a truly biblical theology. He also seeks to relate oriental models of the world to Christianity (see *Creating a Just Future*, pp.87-101).
 The AuSable Institute, Michigan, aims to promote Christian environmental stewardship with a biblical basis. See the collection of essays edited by Wesley Granberg-Michaelson: *Tending the Garden: Essays on the Gospel and the Earth* (Eerdmans, Grand Rapids, Michigan, 1987).

## 5. A CHRISTIAN RESPONSE TO CREATION

Since God is the Creator of the world and has charged men and women with caring for it, and is also himself present and active within nature, Christians have the strongest possible reasons for a sensitive and caring attitude to their fellow creatures. If we think of the human being as steward or priest of creation, we must adopt a respectful and co-operative policy toward nature. This attitude is enhanced and not threatened by a refusal to idolize creation and a determination to worship the Creator alone. Such a balanced position has been exemplified in the Christian tradition by Francis of Assisi (c. 1182-1226), by the Benedictine communities, and by many saints of the Celtic Church and of the East. Edward Echlin quotes many beautiful examples from the Christian tradition of witness to the integrity of creation. He also points to signs of a revival of the valuing of creation by the churches today in face of the contemporary errors of anthropocentrism and false milennialism.[1] We can only suggest briefly here some of the ways in which ecological awareness might be expressed by Christians today.

### (1) Ecological Discipleship

God calls us in the context of our earthly lives. The sins from which we must be saved include the pollution of earth, air and waters, and the waste and misuse of the world's resources.[2] The eternal life which God gives is to be expressed in earthly, physical ways. The future fulfilment of that life is not to be pictured as a bodiless, ethereal abstraction but as the perfection, transformation and glorification of the body and its environment.

Those who are justified by faith and receive in the Holy Spirit a pledge and first instalment of the new life, live now on earth as citizens of heaven. We are not to aim at living a purely 'spiritual' life by abstracting ourselves from the earthiness of our existence. It is this material, physical world that is the arena of God's activity in creation and in grace. We do not become more spiritual by being less physical.

The God to whom we pray is present here, although he is more immediately present in heaven. We pray in our Lord's Prayer that his will be done on earth as in heaven.

### (2) Ethical Imperatives

Christians must join with those who press for sustainable development and who resist the pollution and degradation of the one global home which we share with all earthly creatures. The avoidance of waste and the minimizing of our demands on the environment form part of a Christian lifestyle. Our expenditure on food, clothes and luxuries should be examined in the light of the global distribution of the world's goods, of our duty to hand the earth on to our descendants as we would wish to find it,

---

[1] Edward Echlin, *op. cit.* See also Edward A. Armstrong: *Saint Francis: Nature Mystic* (University of California Press, 1973); Leslie Hardinge, *The Celtic Church in Britain* (SPCK, London, 1972); A. M. Allchin, 'The Theology of Nature in the Eastern Fathers and among Anglican Theologians' in H. Montefiore (ed.) *op. cit.; Daphne D. C. Pochin Mould: The Celtic Saints: Our Heritage* (Clonmore and Reynolds, Ltd., Dublin, 1956); Esther de Waal (ed.): *The Celtic Vision: Prayers and Blessings from the Outer Hebrides* (Darton, Longman and Todd, London 1990).

[2] See Barbara Wood: *Our World, God's World* (Bible Reading Fellowship, London, 1986).

CARING FOR THE EARTH

and of our responsibility to and for other creatures.[1]

Of course Christians should avoid the use of poisons in their own houses and gardens. Where it is absolutely necessary to deal with insect 'invasions', natural substances should be used whenever possible. The requirements of a Christian environmental ethic obviously apply also to agriculture.

Those who do not farm for a living must show understanding of the economic and commercial constraints upon farmers, but at the same time farmers must themselves wrestle with these matters. Implications for diet and animal welfare arising from the conditions in which animals are kept by modern 'factory farming' techniques are outside the scope of this study, but considerations of land use and the distribution of the earth's resources also indicate that we should drastically cut down our consumption of meat. Feeding grain to cattle is wasteful compared with using it to feed people directly, and land set free by a reduction in pasturage could be used to grow crops for human consumption.[2] Mixed organic farming is the best way to safeguard the continued fertility of the soil. In the administration of its own land the Church could encourage this type of agriculture, and even require it upon changes of tenancy.

Christians need to cultivate an awareness of the value of nature which is based on sound theological and ecological foundations, and should then take part in local environmental discussions. Many of these, such as disputes about planning applications for the extraction of inland gas and oil, are complex, involving mixed motives, conflicting arguments and national energy policies which, however regrettable, cannot be changed locally. Nevertheless Christians should not stand aside but should be seen to be concerned. We must be willing to take part in political debate and action, alongside others who care for God's Earth.[3]

### (3) Local Churches

The majority of churches and cathedrals have at least some land attached to them. Many churchyards are sanctuaries for wild life because of the variety of vegetation which grows in them. Few want to see an untidy churchyard, and most people see a well-kept one as an indication that other things also are well cared for. But a measure of diversity in the planting of shrubs, and perhaps the leaving of an uncut bank or verge somewhere, are not inconsistent with tidiness.[4] And surely the churchyard is one place at least where poisons should be banned!

Finally churches can give a lead in encouraging the recycling of paper, aluminium and the like, not only for fund-raising, but for environmental reasons.

[1] See Horace Dammers, *A Christian Life Style* (Hodder and Stoughton, London, 1986).
[2] Andrew Linzey, *Animal Rights* (SCM, London, 1976), pp.35f.
[3] Tim Cooper in *Green Christianity: Caring for the Whole Creation* (Hodder and Stoughton, London, 1990) gives a comprehensive account of the relation between Christianity and Green Politics.
[4] H. Stapleton and P. Burman, *The Churchyards Handbook,* Second Edition (CIO Publishing, London, 1976) pp.4-5. The *Living Churchyard* Project (Church and Conservation Project, Arthur Rank Centre, National Agricultural Centre, Stoneleigh, Kenilworth, Warwickshire, CV8 2LZ) consists of an information pack and a range of audio-visual material to stimulate churches, parish groups, and managers of burial grounds of all kinds to explore the scope for enhancing wildlife and its habitats.

## 6. ECOLOGY AND *FAITH IN THE COUNTRYSIDE*

The Archbishops' Commission on Rural Area (ACORA) has produced its report, *Faith in the Countryside*[1] since the first edition of this Study was published. The Commission's terms of reference were:
1. To examine the effects of economic, environmental and social change on the rural community.
2. To describe the changing nature of the Church in the countryside.
3. To examine the theological factors which bear upon the mission and ministry of the Church in rural areas.
4. In the light of the above, to make recommendations for consideration and action.

The environmental factor is present but is noted only for its effect on people. This anthropocentric approach is consistently followed through and is inevitable given the Commission's starting point.

The theological introduction in chapter 2 begins by recognizing the religious significance of nature. A brief mention is made of the concept of the human being as 'the microcosm of creation', together with an enimatic assertion that such a concept is the opposite of anthropocentric. However this tantalizingly brief statement is not amplified.[2] The Commission follows the Church of Scotland publication *While the Earth Endures*[3] in seeing human beings as stewards, custodians and companions of the non-human world, but adds the model of the human being as priest.[4]

The Report notes the growing realization of the relatedness of humanity to the rest of nature[5], which the authors think is even beginning to affect planning decisions.[6] The 'green audits' undertaken by certain county councils are commended.[7] The references to 'more environmentally-benign husbandry',[8] and organically grown food[9] are positive but restrained, and the low-key treatment of biotechnology seems out of proportion to the momentous issues involved in human modifications to the very structure of creation.[10] The authors judge that the Church of England 'could well see itself coming under pressure to review the nature of its [agricultural] tenancies to reflect theological insights rather than a slavish acceptance of growing intensification and the move to larger units', but they do not themselves seem inclined to exert such pressure.[11] They question the perception of agriculture's problem as being one of surplus land.[12]

---

[1] *Faith in the Countryside: A Report Presented to the Archbishops of Canterbury and York* (Churchman Publishing, Worthing, 1990).
[2] *Faith in the Countryside* 2.27.
[3] *While the Earth Endures: A Report on the Theological and Ethical Considerations of Responsible Land-Use in Scotland* (Society, Religion and Technology Project, Edinburgh, 1986).
[4] *Faith in the Countryside*, 2.22-25.
[5] *Ibid.* 4.3.
[6] *Ibid.* 4.10.
[7] *Ibid.* 4.23, 5.36.
[8] *Ibid.* 4.25.
[9] *Ibid.* 4.28.
[10] *Ibid.* 4.27.
[11] *Ibid.* 5.54.
[12] *Ibid.* 5.56.

More widespread take-up of the Farm Woodlands Scheme[1], and compensation for voluntarily reduced stocking limits in upland areas to safeguard their ecology,[2] are urged. The Report deplores the lack of a broad-based assessment of the social, environmental and economic impact of motorways.[3] The authors of the Report recognize the need for more government money to be made available to further ecological objectives.[4] The Church also should budget for a greater emphasis on the social and environmental aspects of investment policy.[5]

In the Chapter on 'Spirituality and Worship' the religious significance of 'wilderness' is recognized, and under 'Mission, Evangelism and Community' it is noted that, according to the Rural Church Project, 78% of Anglicans 'thought that the Church should be "involved in environmental issues".'[6] The Report suggests that the environmental impact of the way we use church buildings should be considered,[7] and the importance of churchyards as conservation areas is noted. Appendix C, 'Conservation and Environmental Pressures on the Countryside' by Dr. Michael Winter,[8] begins with a useful analysis of 'traditional' and 'radical' environmentalism and demonstrates, among other things, the inadequacy of existing measures for the conservation of the countryside.

The most resounding ecological statement of the whole Report is to be found, strangely, in the Chapter on Ministry, where the authors state boldly that a further aspect needs adding to the statement of the Lambeth Bishops concerning the mission of the Church. They write:
> 'Mission is not only concerned with the structures of human society, but with the nature of the universe itself. The ecological debate is at heart a theological one and needs to the accepted as such by the Church at large, and not just by those in rural areas or with a particular environmental concern. A fifth aim might be added:
> 5. To assert the cosmic significance of the Gospel.'[9]

If only this aim had been allowed to inform the whole Report more wholeheartedly, we should have had a far more passionate advocacy of the imperative to care for the Earth.

---

[1] *Ibid.* 5.58.
[2] *Ibid.* 5.62.
[3] *Ibid.* 5.97.
[4] *Ibid.* 4.25, 5.45-46.
[5] *Ibid.* 12.30, 5.54, 12.40-43, 12.52.
[6] *Ibid.* 11.55.
[7] *Ibid.* 12.93.
[8] *Ibid.* pp.335ff.
[9] *Ibid.* 8.11. The other aims quoted from the Lambeth Conference are: '1. To proclaim the Good News of the Kingdom. 2. To teach, baptize, and nurture new believers. 3. To respond to human need by loving service. 4. To transform unjust structures in society.'